AF477067

WILTSHIRE

A Photographic Record 1840–1920

WILTSHIRE

A Photographic Record 1840–1920

MICHAEL MARSHMAN

COUNTRYSIDE BOOKS

NEWBURY, BERKSHIRE

First Published 1982
© Michael Marshman 1982
All rights reserved. No reproduction permitted without the prior permission of the publishers:
Countryside Books
3 Catherine Road,
Newbury, Berkshire

ISBN 0 905392 18 3

Designed by Mon Mohan

Typeset by Robcroft Ltd, London WC1
Printed in England

I would like to dedicate this book to my late father,
Charles Marshman, who taught me to be a photographer.

Acknowledgements

I am very grateful to the many individuals and organizations who have allowed me to copy photographs in their possession over a period of several years. For the selection of pictures used in this book I would like to express my thanks to the following:

The Aethelstan Museum, Malmesbury, pages 43, 63, 65, 74, 78, 82, 86
Mr Peter A. J. Brown 29, 50, 53, 63, 69, 76, 77, 83
Mrs Dorothy Chivers 23
Cricklade Historical Society 17, 24, 34, 63, 72
Devizes Library, Wiltshire Library & Museum Service 30, 33, 57, 71
The Fox Talbot Museum of Photography, Lacock 13, 37
Mr Michael Lansdown 15, 18, 38, 53, 54
Mr Peter Maundrell 42, 55
Melksham & District Historical Association 19, 45, 75
Mr Roger Pope 27, 57, 66, 95
Mr Ken Rogers 48, 50, 61, 81, 93
Salisbury & South Wiltshire Museum 26, 36, 49, 50, 51, 58, 61, 70, 71, 92
Mr Mike Stone 61, 63, 65, 66
Swindon Library, Wiltshire Library & Museum Service 14, 18, 40, 44, 46, 47, 51, 59, 64, 68, 69, 72
Trowbridge Library, Wiltshire Library & Museum Service 21, 26, 30, 43, 94
Wiltshire Archaeological & Natural History Society 8, 16, 17, 21, 22, 25, 29, 31, 34, 39, 75, 80, 86
Wiltshire Record Office 18, 20, 32, 48, 55, 69, 79, 83, 84, 85, 89
Wiltshire Regimental Museum 90, 92
Wootton Bassett Historical Society 79, 88
The Yelde Hall Museum, Chippenham 26, 32, 44, 45, 49, 53, 56, 60, 77, 87, 95

I would also like to thank all the staff of libraries and museums and the honourary officers of societies, who have patiently helped me during my photographic work. For help with information I would especially like to express my thanks to, Dr John Chandler, John D'Arcy, Michael Lansdown, Robert Lassam, Lesley Marshman, Ken Rogers, and Roger Traherne.

I would also like to thank the publishers, Nicholas and Suzanne Battle, for allowing me the opportunity to publish material that I have been accumulating for some years.

Contents

Introduction

FOR many years Wiltshire has been a county through which people passed with no more than an overnight stop. Whether travelling west, to Devon and Cornwall, or east, to London, by stage coach or train, there seemed little to cause the traveller to stay. The major routes of road and rail are designed to take people to large centres of population or to holiday resorts, so that for many, Wiltshire is a landscape, a town, a village or a cathedral spire seen briefly through a window.

It was not always so. In prehistoric times the area, now known as Wiltshire, was comparatively densely populated and today can boast the largest number of known archaeological sites of any county. Every succeeding historical period has also left some legacy to our landscape, straight Roman roads, Saxon towns, Norman castles and markets, medieval street plans, enclosure hedges and landscaped estates. The pattern of life had evolved slowly with no radical upheaval until the end of the eighteenth century, when industrialization began to take effect causing a very marked movement from village to town in many areas.

Wiltshire is not a cohesive topographical unit. In fact the saying, "As different as chalk from cheese", probably comes from the differences within the county. The chalk, Salisbury Plain and the Marlborough Downs, supported vast flocks of sheep, which in turn fertilized the thin soil with the help of good management in their folding. The cheese is the clay lowlands in the north and west, traditionally a land of small farmers, meadows and dairying. There was a religious difference too, in that the landlords and big farmers of the chalklands tended to support the church and the establishment, while the small farmers and labourers on the clay were more likely to be chapel folk and non-comformists.

These areas are often closer in their attitudes to adjacent counties than to each other. Salisbury Plain is tilted to the south and focuses on Salisbury which, in its turn, looks towards Hampshire and Southampton. The five towns of West Wiltshire, Bradford on Avon, Melksham, Trowbridge, Westbury and Warminster follow the line of the Somerset border and would regard Bath as their chief town instead of Salisbury or Swindon. Chippenham, Calne, Corsham and especially Malmesbury are on the fringes of the Cotswolds while the towns of the north, such as Wootton Bassett and Marlborough, will turn to Swindon, which itself looks towards Oxford and London. Near the centre of the county stands Devizes, an ancient town but one which various circumstances denied any opportunity of developing and drawing all parts of the county inwards. Even recently, with the formation of the County Council in 1889, it was Trowbridge on the western edge of Wiltshire that was eventually chosen as the administrative capital. The respective historical and geographical claims of Salisbury and Devizes were not sufficient, for it seemed that Trowbridge was the only town that could be reached easily by rail from all other parts of the county.

Until very recently the majority of people obtained their living directly from the land, whether as landowner, farmer or labourer. The pattern of farming had not greatly changed and the enclosures of common land probably caused less upheaval than in many other counties, such as those of the Midlands. During the nineteenth century improved methods of farming became available, including land drainage and reclamation, better soil fertility and varieties of seed and improved agricultural implements. All these were enthusiastically taken up by many local farmers. Wiltshire also pioneered much agricultural machinery through such firms as Brown and May of Devizes, Robert and John Reeves of Bratton, and John Wallis Titt of Warminster.

Initially the period was one of agricultural prosperity in corn, sheep and dairying, but this came to an end in 1870 when many factors combined to bring about a severe depression. A succession of wet, cold springs meant poor harvests, while imported North American corn caused a fall in prices. Much arable land was put down to grass but unfortunately the price of wool was also falling while the wet weather caused foot-rot in sheep and liver-rot in cattle. Cheap imports of cheese made more farmers turn to milk production as cheese and butter making on the farm became unprofitable. This slump lasted until 1914 when war meant that much more home produced food was required and farmers were able to enjoy more prosperous times. By this time however the traditional pattern of farming had greatly changed.

Meanwhile the growth of industry in many towns had resulted in the depopulation of their neighbouring villages as rural labourers crowded into the urban areas to find work in the new factories. The chief industry of Wiltshire was cloth, but after 1825 that woollen trade began to decrease. Even so, in 1841 out of a total population of just over 250,000, 6,000 people were either weavers or connected with the industry in some way. The effects of mechanization of this industry had been great, as can be seen by the increase of population in the mill town of Trowbridge, from 6,075 in 1811 to 9,545 in 1821. In general, however, the nineteenth century was a period of gradual decline interspersed by slight recoveries. In 1842 there were 25 manufacturers in Trowbridge, by 1903 only 5 mills remained.

Many other local industries were based on farming, the Wilts United Dairy and the Anglo-Swiss Condensed Milk Co., C. & T. Harris (Calne) Ltd. and Bowyers of Trowbridge for bacon, while tanning and glovemaking were both of local importance. The best Bath stone came from the Box Hill area of Wiltshire while iron ore was worked at Seend and Westbury.

The aspect of northern Wiltshire was greatly changed by the siting of the Great Western Railway Works at Swindon. The decision was reached in 1840 and the works had been built and brought into operation by January 1843. In 1846 Swindon built its first engines for Brunel and Sir Daniel Gooch. In later years items other than locomotives, such as cast iron bridges, were built. The rise of Swindon was meteoric. In 1831 the population had been 1,742, it reached 4,879 in 1851 and 45,006 by 1901.

The development of the railway system had a largely beneficial effect on the community, making the movement of both people and produce easier than ever before and opening up new markets and places of employment. The effects on roads and canals were not so helpful. The Kennet and Avon Canal and the Wilts and Berks Canal had been important waterways, but they were unable to survive railway competition and by the end of the nineteenth century there was very little canal traffic. The effects on the roads of the turnpike trusts were uneven and some roads even increased in usage, acting as feeders to the railways. However the trusts were doomed by the Highways Act of 1862 and none survived in Wiltshire after 1879. Road traffic continued but, where the railway was an alternative, most goods travelled by train.

The pattern of small market towns, with their dependant villages, was changing in the west and north of the county into one of manufacturing towns and shrinking villages, whose inhabitants still worked the land to supply the townspeople. This was a less stable partnership than the traditional one, as the towns swallowed not only the agricultural produce of the countryside, but also most of its young people who were attracted by the higher wages, entertainments and educational opportunities on offer. This effect was little felt in the eastern and southern parts where agriculture and its associated industries remained the predominant occupations. Communities such as Marlborough and Salisbury retained their role of market centres.

From 1820 onwards the rapidly expanding populations of many towns created the need for a massive programme of housebuilding. Whole streets and estates were financed by one person, mainly providing dwellings for artisans and factory workers in the west and for railway workers in Swindon. Streets of terraced back to back houses sprang up, with the bulk of the building taking place between 1840 and 1880.

At the same time as the concentration of workers in towns was creating this demand, the increased prosperity of those towns led to the building of many villas for the manufacturing, business and professional classes. Many towns have Victorian villas on their outskirts with ribbon development along major roads. During this time there was also a movement among the more wealthy townspeople to move out and purchase country houses or small estates.

One other factor changed Wiltshire while, at the same time, fossilizing much of its landscape. This was the taking over of a large part of Salisbury Plain by the War Office. There had always been a military presence with the local Volunteers, Militia and the Wiltshire Regiment. Cavalry had been brought in and stationed at Trowbridge to control unrest among cloth workers and Chartists in that area. This new phase was to have far reaching results and began in 1897 with the purchase of 60 square miles of Plain for £450,000. Some towns, such as Warminster, virtually became garrison towns while many villages, such as Sutton Veny, were dramatically altered by the proximity of large army camps. Despite the space taken by tank and grenade ranges much of the original landscape has been preserved and although havoc has been wrought by tracked vehicles there are still places where Wiltshire flora and fauna flourishes.

This changing scene in Wiltshire was captured by many photographers, but none with a national reputation. Although his home at Lacock Abbey provided his base for photographic experiments, William Henry Fox Talbot does not seem to have photographed many Wiltshire subjects. Rightfully acknowledged as the 'father of British Photography', he is commemorated by a splendid museum situated in a large stone barn at the very gates of his country seat.

We owe most of our pictorial records to local commercial and amateur photographers, many of whom are now unknown and forgotten. Of those whose work we can still identify are, W. Hooper of Swindon, F. Holmes of Mere, Alfred Burgess of Market Lavington and Joseph Hunt of Calne.

Another well known photographer was Wilkinson, the 'postcard king' of Trowbridge, who produced thousands of views of Wiltshire towns and villages and extended his activities into the surrounding counties and the Midlands. Unfortunately in the 1950s many tons of his glass negatives had to be destroyed because there was no space available for, and little public interest in, their preservation.

An amateur photographer, whose work has fortunately survived, in Devizes Museum, was Arthur Mitchell. He was the Relieving Officer for No. 1 Devizes District and was responsible for running the workhouse. One of his hobbies was photographing the people and scenes he saw as he travelled through the nearby villages. The photographs that he took of country people around Devizes provide one of our best records of rural life at the turn of the century.

It is to these people, and the many unknown camera users, that we owe the pictorial records of our recent past. Negatives and photographs are fragile objects, easily destroyed and often difficult to preserve, and many interesting photographs are now so faded or damaged as to be beyond reproduction. It is therefore important to preserve and copy those that remain, and much good work is being done in this field by individuals, societies and museums. These photographs provide our link with a vanished way of life, one that was lived by our grandparents and great grandparents, but one that is so far removed from our present state as to seem centuries old. The impression of this life that is conveyed by one old photograph can often be worth several thousand words.

Lacock Abbey was the home, from 1826, of William Henry Fox Talbot, the father of British photography. It was in the Abbey and grounds that Fox Talbot pursued his experiments on the light sensitivity of various chemicals which were to result in the first photographic negative in August 1835. This was of a small latticed window taken from inside the Abbey with the aid of a camera obscura. From this he developed his calotype process which he patented in 1841. This picture of the Abbey is an early calotype of 1842 from across the River Avon.

The Calotype of 'The Ladder' appeared in Fox Talbot's book, *The Pencil of Nature*. Beneath the picture he wrote, 'When the sun shines, small portraits can be obtained by my process in one or two seconds, but large portraits require a somewhat longer time. When the weather is dark and cloudy a corresponding allowance is necessary and a greater demand is made upon the patience of the sitter. Groups of figures require no longer time to obtain than single features would require, since the camera depicts them all at once, however numerous they may be, but at present we cannot well succeed in this branch of art without some previous concern and arrangement. But when a group of persons has been artistically arranged, and trained by a little practice to maintain absolute immobility for a few seconds of a time, very delightful pictures are easily obtained.' The picture was taken in 1841.

(above) Swindon's best known photographer was William Hooper, seen here outside his first photographic studio at 2 Market Street. He worked from c1903 to c1922 and has left some splendid photographs as his legacy to future generations. As an acknowledged expert in child portraiture Hooper must have photographed large numbers of Edwardian families as well as producing his townscapes and landscapes which we find of such great interest. Hooper himself had a penchant for being photographed outside his later studio at 6 Cromwell Street, normally with the motorcycle and wickerwork sidecar on which he, his assistant and their equipment travelled to their venues. Hooper was only one month later than Holmes in photographing a flash of lightning, which he achieved at 1.15 a.m. on 24th June 1906 from the roof of his studio.

(see page 8) A desire of many photographers was that of being the first to succeed in capturing a flash of lightning on a photographic plate. One of the first to achieve this was Frederick Holmes, of Mere, in May 1906 when he took this picture of lightning entering the ground 56 yards from the church tower. While Holmes was using his cumbersome equipment the storm lasted from 3.30 p.m. to 10.30 p.m. and he would have later learned that both the obelisk at Stourhead and the Church of St. James at Shaftesbury had been struck. Holmes was also a good businessman as can be seen in an extract from The Photographic Monthly for August 1906. Headed 'A Postcard Triumph' it says, 'F. Holmes, of Mere, Wiltshire, photographed a flash of lightning which appeared to strike near the tower of the local church. He had it postcarded in half tone, and sold 20,000 in 15 days.

Wiltshire Childhood

THE child's world was one of a small, enclosed community bounded by family and friends within the town or village. There were few opportunities to travel far afield and, for a village child, a trip to the nearest market town was as exciting as one to London for the youngster of today. Life was somewhat parochial and when in a neighbouring community a child would feel slightly ill at ease, he would realise that he was a 'foreigner' in the eyes of the locals.

Until the passing of the 1870 Education Act primary education was very uneven and many country children were employed on the farm from an early age, often as bird scarers or as tenders of pastured animals. Wiltshire towns, however, saw less child labour than their northern counterparts as the declining local woollen industry provided less and less employment.

Families were large, infant disease and mortality high and many children lived with their parents in two and three room cottages, often with families of 8 or 9 sleeping in the same small airless room. For other families, more fortunate and prosperous, life was entirely different. The 'Two Nations' of Disraeli were much more in evidence in rural areas than in many cities, and landowners and farmers lived in completely different worlds to the one of their labourers.

However childhood, whether with homemade toys or formal parties, was full of delights and suprises. If the country child had no toys, there was bird nesting, fishing, apple scrumping and many other enjoyable pursuits. The town child might live in an insanitary house in a narrow court but there were hoops, hopscotch and conkers to be played and pleasure in the company of his fellows.

Most poor children from the towns would have been familiar with the local soup kitchen, which had usually been established by a local philanthrophist 'for the feeding of the poor'. The one in The Conigre in Trowbridge had been set up by Hannah Gouldsmith in 1888. This picture, c1903, shows a wide variety of utensils used by the children for carrying the soup or broth home to their hungry families. Often local landowners would send meat to the soup kitchen; in Trowbridge Mrs Clark of Bellefield House sent vension from her deer park every Christmas and Easter.

(above) The greatest influence on young girls was their mother. From here they learned the domestic tasks that they would need to perform, either as housewives in their own right, or as maids if they were to go into service at the local 'big house' or vicarage. In an age when self sufficiency was more of a necessity than an alternative life style the gathering of harvests from hedge and wood was an important part of the household routine. In their season mushrooms, gooseberries, crab apples, sloes, blackberries and nuts would have all been collected for the Wiltshire kitchen. This charming picture, taken in 1905 at Allington near Devizes, probably shows the start of just such a foray after the fruits of the hedgerow.

(opposite top right) The village, with its surrounding fields and woods, was the entire world of the country child. He would know that area, its people, birds and animals intimately. At this time, with no instant access to wider events and places, the family maintained its traditional role as a close knit unit. An important part of this unit was the grandparents, who would almost certainly live in a neighbouring village if not the same one as their grandchildren. The children were frequent visitors and this small boy, at his grandparents in All Cannings, c1905, has been helping to pick apples which are now safely held in his grandmother's capacious apron.

16

(below) Many children helped their parents by working from an early age. This was most common in rural areas or where the father was self employed. The most obvious case was on the farm where the employment of his sons in the fields and his daughters in the dairy would often save the farmer the cost of a labourer or two. In Cricklade Jack Stephen takes young Phyllis Cuss for a ride while driving the pony and trap for his father Barry, the local dairyman.

The playground of the town child was the dusty streets and, if he were lucky, a nearby canal or river. The toys and playthings were often made at home. In this picture two boys hold hoops while two others seem to have whips with which they would have lashed tops up to 20 yards through the air. These latter were sometimes slotted so that they hummed whilst travelling and all continued to spin on reaching the ground. This corner of Cheltenham Street would have been a popular place for a Swindon child as Niblett & Co. sold ginger beer and lemonade in marble stoppered bottles. The business was established in Swindon during the early 1880s and this photograph is probably c1890.

Many schools were built and endowed for poor children while others kept free places for the less well off. Wilton Park School was endowed in 1838 by Lady Georgina Herbert for the education and clothing of 35 poor girls. This photograph was taken in 1903 when Miss Margaret Aikman was schoolmistress. The girls wear pinafores which were provided as a uniform and also carry staves which they probably used in various exercises.

Birthday and Christmas parties, whether they were small family gatherings or grander affairs such as this Edwardian fancy dress party, generated much excitement in both the anticipation and the event. The children involved here come from many of the prominent families in Trowbridge and doubtless the proceedings, well supervised by adults, were rather more formal than if the participants had been left to their own entertainments.

The stone laying ceremony for a new school would not always have been a cause for juvenile celebration but a half day holiday to attend such an event was enough to make these Melksham children cheer. As a part of the improvement in educational standards the old British School, with its 275 pupils, had been taken over by Wiltshire County Council in 1909. Later that year this red brick school was built in Lowbourne on a site adjacent to the old building.

Rural Life

I N Wiltshire most people lived in the country and the greater number of them were poor. An inquiry into English agriculture made in 1850–51, by Sir James Caird, states the diet of a typical Salisbury Plain labourer; breakfast, flour with a little butter and water; mid-day, bread with cheese (the latter only if he had no young family to keep); afternoon, a few potatoes with bacon if he could afford it; supper, bread and water. Richard Jefferies, writing 20 years later, said that the diet of the Wiltshire labourer was chiefly bread and cheese.

On the brighter side there were cottagers who were better off and farms where the labourers ate at the farmhouse and beer and cider was available. Then there were farmers and yeomen whose standard of living was much better, with plenty of food, well proportioned houses and good furniture which had often been handed down from generation to generation. It is this better side of life that most contemporary photographs show, tending to paint a rosy picture of a well ordered and pleasant life.

While the poor were in the majority, the village community itself was varied. Most were self sufficient with blacksmiths, carpenters, wheelwrights, millers, carriers and shopkeepers. Many were visited by tinkers and pedlars who sold items otherwise unobtainable except in the larger towns. In all there were farmers, landowners, servants and clerics to produce a balanced and stable pattern of life.

The overriding factor of rural life was the lack of change with events being as fixed as the seasons. Because of the regular pattern years were often remembered by exceptional occasions such as fire, floods and multiple births in animals. Being such a part of the natural world the countryman was alive to the changing weather and seasons. Summer was hard and hot work in the dusty fields, Autumn with its shortening days gave a sense of drawing in, Winter was a time to be dreaded with little food and warmth, wet and freezing working conditions and no light in the evenings, while Spring was a time of awakening and relief at having survived the winter.

Downton corn mill, in 1885, presented a pleasant rural scene. The mill had always been an integral part of the English countryside and retained its importance throughout the nineteenth century. At Downton the miller, who was also a maltster, was George Athey who had probably taken over the tenancy of the mill in 1881. Just intruding, on the righthand side of the picture, is the more modern building that housed a paper mill while out of sight on the left was a tannery.

The farmer and his wife lived fairly isolated lives, their only visitors being other farmers (mainly on Sundays), salesmen, pedlars and valuers. This couple, the farmer in his mud splattered gaiters, have probably just returned from an infrequent trip into the nearby market town of Devizes from their village of All Cannings, c1905. At this time the annual income of a small farmer was quite low but much of their food was home produced, their personal expenses were small, they did not need to keep up with clothing fashions and most household furniture and equipment had been inherited.

A popular winter event was the meet of the local foxhounds. The short days of winter did not provide much time for entertainment and such an occurrence was a welcome break from the monotony of cold, hard work. The hunt was not only for the wealthy, although this was the only class who rode; anyone could follow hounds on foot or by bicycle. The most sacred preserves were open to the hunt and for fear of the social consequences few landowners would bar their gates, so the countryman could gain access to all his surroundings. Indeed even gamekeepers were powerless if they apprehended well known poachers when the hounds were about and a ready made excuse was therefore at hand. This meet at The Black Horse, Cherhill, was in 1908.

Before the coming of steam, windmills were a fairly common sight on the chalklands where there were no powerful streams to drive watermills. Few survived into the twentieth century and this one at Tilshead can be seen to be very derelict when it was acquired by Mr G. Watson Taylor in 1907. Although he demolished the ruin, his intentions were of the best as he gave the oak beams for the restoration of the chancel roof of the local parish church of St Thomas à Beckett. This windmill was a Wiltshire post mill with a thatched roof and worked with two common, and two shuttered sails.

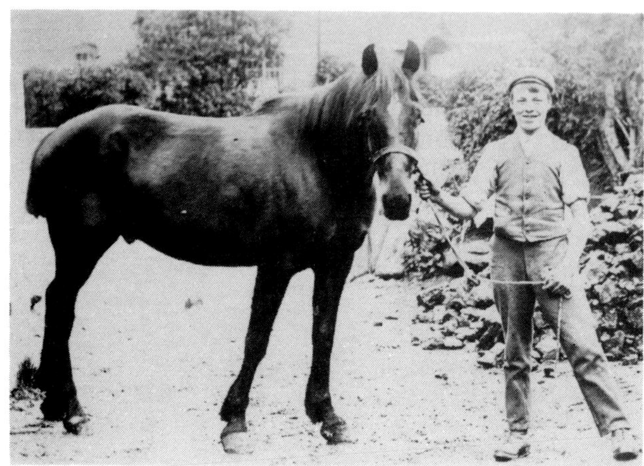

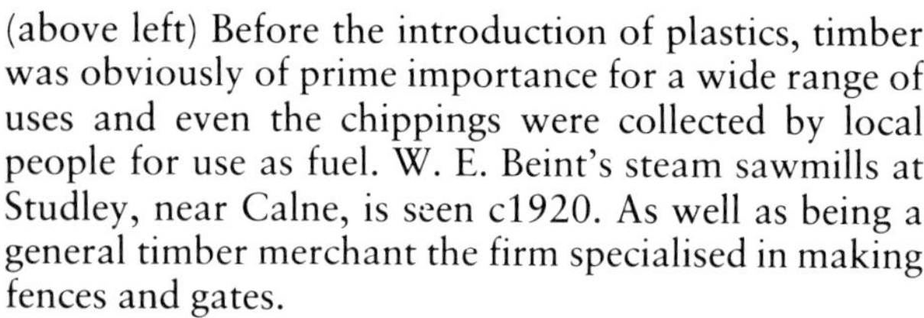

(above left) Before the introduction of plastics, timber was obviously of prime importance for a wide range of uses and even the chippings were collected by local people for use as fuel. W. E. Beint's steam sawmills at Studley, near Calne, is seen c1920. As well as being a general timber merchant the firm specialised in making fences and gates.

(above right) The most important animal in the country was the horse. On the farm the best paid labourers were the horsemen and carters, for until steam power had been harnessed for agricultural use his was the only power other than oxen. Transport on the roads was by horse and the coach drivers were kings of the road while in the country houses coachmen and grooms occupied a prominent position. This stablelad, with his cheeky grin, is obviously well pleased with the turn out of this well proportioned stallion at All Cannings.

(right) Many housewives still baked their own bread but even in isolated villages the baker was making his appearance. At Horton, near Devizes c1905, the local baker and his young assistant proudly display their finished product and one of the tools of their trade, a long handled wooden oven peel which was used for taking loaves from the fierce heat of the oven.

(right) Apart from use as a building material, chalk was required for producing whitening, much in demand by the housewife for doorsteps, hearths, window ledges and walls. The whitening ring at Calstone was 18 feet in diameter and within it the chalk was crushed in water by the horse drawn roller until a paste was formed. This paste was moulded into balls, pictured in the wheelbarrow, and hardened in the sun. Edwin Green was the whitening manufacturer here from the 1880s until well into the twentieth century.

(below) In 1900 Oxford Street, in Ramsbury, presented the typically evocative scene that we expect from the photographs of this period. Most of the houses are thatched and many are timber framed and medieval in origin. One of the chief dangers with thatch was the risk of fire; several villages, such as nearly Aldbourne, had been partially destroyed more than once by flames leaping from one burning roof to the next. Many villages possessed long handled hooks for removing burning thatch, those at West Lavington are still in existence.

(above left and right) One of the most important social institutions of any village was the public house. Although still a largely male dominated stronghold at this time, thus denying access to half the adult population, it was club, debating place and games room, as well as a place to drink beer and cider, to the men of the community. The inn had not been designed for this, but over the centuries had evolved from the traveller's rest place and village drinking den into the meeting place for the community. These two photographs were taken at The King's Head in the market town of Cricklade in 1880. The interior picture shows 5 men with their jug of ale and long clay churchwarden pipes. In the scene outside the inn the landlord is serving two card players with beer from a glazed jug. The beer cost $1\frac{1}{2}$d a pint or one shilling (5p) a gallon and the tobacco was 1d an ounce.

(right) Before 1839 the policing of rural Wiltshire had been undertaken by petty or parish constables. Throughout the nineteenth century special constables were also sworn in by local magistrates, as was Robert Clark at Leigh near Ashton Keynes. This photograph is difficult to date and could be from the 1840s and is probably no later than the 1850s.

Many villages possessed their own roadmender, who would fill pot holes with flint or chalk and sometimes make more extensive repairs. He was often paid by the parish and doubtless had a poor, but not a lonely existence for he would meet all the travellers. This roadman, whose wages were about 8 shillings (40p) a week, was from Horton, near Devizes, c1905. The knees of his corduroy trousers are patched, an indication of much time spent in kneeling on hard surfaces.

Home for the country man was usually a small cottage, often thatched, with a garden that he could cultivate in the light summer evening after a long day's work. This tidy cottage, near Devizes c1905, is well thatched and has a modern porch of corrugated iron. The wallpaper has a bold floral pattern while the window still holds geraniums in earthenware pots. The front garden contains a rosemary bush in the bottom right hand corner of the picture. Rosemary was used for flavouring the lard, which was produced after fat from the cottager's pig had been rendered down. Many families kept a pig, feeding it on scraps from the kitchen and milk products and normally killing it around Christmas time.

(above left) From the end of the nineteenth century the windpump became a common sight in the English landscape. The most common usage was for pumping water, as with this example near Chippenham, although it was also used for grinding corn and generating electricity. Often water was pumped for distances of up to a mile to a reservoir or isolated building.

(above right) In the Salisbury area, especially around Winterslow, truffle hunting was a profitable occupation. Eli Collins was well known, both in England and on the continent, as an expert truffle hunter. His dogs, which were of Spanish descent with traces of poodle, located the truffles by smell whereupon Eli would dig them up using his short iron shod stick. Truffles, which are underground fungi, are in season from October to January and a good dog could find up to 8 lbs in a day. In 1901 a truffle the size of a globe artichoke was worth 6d (2½p).

26

(opposite bottom right) Most villagers kept at least one pig, which was often killed on the premises by the local butcher, or at the home of the nearby pig killer. This scene at Market Lavington is in the garden of 3 High Street, the home of Mr Ward, on the far left, who was the pig killer in 1915. A pig killing was a bit of an event with a few jars of cider among the neighbours and often a small sweepstake on the weight of the pig. The seemingly barbaric practice of burning the pig, depicted here, was merely the means of removing the bristles after the pig had been humanely despatched.

Village post offices possessed surprisingly large numbers of staff and provided very efficient collection and delivery services in both urban and rural areas. In 1910 Pewsey Post Office had a staff of 24, some of whom are pictured here, including 2 messenger boys.

Farming

FARMING was basically of two types. The chalk downs were given over to large flocks of sheep, whose shepherds would often see no living beings other than their sheep for days on end. The life of the Wiltshire shepherd has been well recorded in W.H. Hudson's 'A Shepherd's Life' and was hard but rewarding work. In the low-lands, dairying and livestock rearing prevailed with small farms and fields.

Much of the farming of the nineteenth century was of a very high standard with good yields, even that most critical observer, William Cobbett, had enthused over the farming in the valley of the Salisbury Avon in 1826. Wiltshire farmers were enthusiastic improvers with new strains of corn, better crosses between old breeds of animals, more intensive cultivation and improved machinery and equipment.

For much of the time the only power on the farm was man and the horse. The horse was of prime importance as nearly every job required his muscles. Later, steam power was used for threshing and ploughing. Work on the farm was varied and although a man might be employed as a carter or stockman, he was expected to turn his hand to any job. Most work needed specialized skills that were often handed down from one generation to the next and took many years to perfect. Laying hedges, making hurdles and gates, doctoring sick animals and repairing machinery were all extra tasks that could crop up during the farming year.

Work on the farm was hard, labourers often rose before dawn and worked for most of the hours of daylight. A ploughman would walk between 9 and 12 miles while at harvest time the working day was from dawn to dusk and the liquid intake, in terms of cider, was enormous. Despite the romantic view of work on the land before the invention of the internal combustion engine, few countrymen would wish to return to the old days when the hours were long, the pay poor, living conditions squalid and the food barely enough to sustain a working man.

(above) Although the chemical fertilizer industry was established in 1840, in 1905 Wiltshire farmers still knew and believed that one of the best ways of enriching the land was by spreading dung over it. At Allington, near Devizes, the muck carts carried their loads from stock yards to fields in the early spring. The muck heap in the yard had been steadily growing all winter as both cattle and horses were fed on hay and cattle cake and now was the time to return all this goodness to the land.

(right) After the decline of weaving as a cottage industry in the seventeenth century the Bromham area had become well known for market gardening. The light friable soil was ideal and produce was supplied to many local towns during the nineteenth and twentieth centuries. Here a good crop of potatoes is being lifted on Sandridge Hill c1900.

Farm labourer Ambrose Matthews and his wife pictured at the door of their Bratton cottage in 1900. Ambrose is wearing traditional Wiltshire labourer's dress of a smock frock with corduroy trousers and a billycock hat. His wages were between 10 and 14 shillings (50 to 70p) a week. His wife is wearing the woman's traditional working dress of a black bodice, a skirt covered by an apron and a sun bonnet.

Windmills and watermills were once common sights but the use of animal power to drive machinery was rarer. This donkey wheel at Broad Hinton was used for pumping water. It was a large thatched structure of wood and stone protecting a treadmill with a wheel of 10 to 12 feet diameter.

After ploughing, the land was harrowed to break up the heavy sods of earth. In 1905 on the banks of the Kennet and Avon canal at Bishop's Cannings a chain harrow, drawn by two horses, is in use on a sunny winter day. By the end of the day the youth would have picked up several pounds of mud on his boots as he slowly lifted them from the soil while following his horses. Working in winter meant using all the hours of daylight, so the horses were fed and groomed in the darkness before breakfast and at the end of the day, about 3.30 to 4.00 p.m., the horses required cleaning, grooming and feeding before the horseman could go to his supper.

(opposite top) Accidents on the farm were sometimes as common as in heavy industry. On Saturday 10th March 1889 a steam driven threshing machine exploded on Belcombe Farm at Bradford on Avon. One man, Mr Jones of Hinton Charterhouse in Somerset, was blown to pieces while another was seriously injured.

(opposite bottom) Sheep shearing was carried out by highly skilled contract gangs who could work extremely quickly and moved from farm to farm during shearing time. The contracts were arranged between farmer and gang leader some weeks before work commenced. When shearing the men worked long hours in hot and uncomfortable conditions and farmers were required to supply a great deal of cider and beer for refreshment. The men were given pocket money while shearing but on the final night a share out of wages was held at a special feast, sometimes called Black Ram Night. The women in this picture would have rolled and packed the fleeces.

(below) Before sheep were shorn they were washed during the early summer to remove the dirt from their fleeces. The fast flowing chalk stream, the Stradbrook at Bratton, is being used for this purpose in 1900 while the flock of black faced sheep in the background are penned in wicker hurdles. The sheep were brought down from Salisbury Plain for this annual event.

(left) Under the Diseases of Animals Act 1894 and 1896 local authorities were required to investigate possible outbreaks of disease. This investigation of foot and mouth at Cricklade, c1902, obviously proved positive and the infected pigs are about to be buried. The gentleman, second from the right would appear to be one of the veterinary inspectors who were called in by Wiltshire County Council for such outbreaks. The pigs were buried in quicklime taken from the barrel on the right.

(below) The best known part of the farming year was haymaking time and many romantic notions of this were cherished by the townsman. In practice it involved long days of hard work by men, women and children to cut, turn and gather the crop while the weather was dry and hot so that the hay for winter feed was sweet and would not go sour in the rick. This Wiltshire wagon is being used at Chittoe in 1901 and all 8 men in the picture have the name John.

Country House and Country Cottage

THE immense gulf between rich and poor in the countryside can be well seen by contrasting the country house with the country cottage. The country house, with its vast armies of servants, landscaped gardens, farms and estates could be a self contained world, having little contact with its poorer neighbours. The cottager, with his large family, often lived in two rooms with an outdoor privy shared by other families. Few photographs were taken of this type of dwelling, the cottages in this section tend to have been the former residences of small farmers and yeomen which were now used to house farm labourers.

Much of Wiltshire was divided into large estates with many tenant farmers and a large army of labourers working for the estate or the farmer. The country has many fine stately homes including Longleat, Stourhead, Ramsbury Manor, Littlecote; Longford Castle, Wardour Castle, Charlton Park and Corsham Court. Many of these big estates and several of the smaller ones built model estate houses for their workers. These can be identified in many areas because of the similarity of their construction.

The traditional Wiltshire cottage was in two forms, one on the chalk was normally thatched while on the clay could be found one with a roof of clay pantiles or stone slates. There are many local variations, but in general terms the former area contains buildings of brick, brick and timber and brick and flint while those in the latter are often of stone. One of the best known stone built villages is the picturesque Castle Combe, but the county contains many other little known, but beautiful villages and attractive cottages.

Like Elizabeth I, Edward VII was very fond of visiting his subjects in their country mansions. In 1908 it was the turn of the Earl and Countess of Pembroke to receive him at Wilton House, between June 27th and 29th. The Salisbury area was a favoured place for many important visitors, containing as it does, the Cathedral, Stonehenge, Longford Castle and other notable sites as well as a racecourse.

The large country vicarage was often home to the gentry although the incumbent and his family were sometimes looked down on by the residents at the 'big house'. The vicarage of Imber, c1910, is especially interesting as it has now been destroyed along with the whole village, apart from the church, after the area became an army training ground in the Second World War. The village was very isolated and was said to be snowed up more often than any other in southern England. The vicar needed to be hardy to visit his outlying parishioners on Salisbury Plain during bad winters, while his family relied greatly on their own company and amusements.

36

'The Group' was a Fox Talbot calotype of his family and friends taken at Lacock Abbey in the early 1840s. There is an atmosphere of a harvest home and the vegetables gathered from the kitchen garden are varied, including carrots, marrows and lettuce, while the seated lady holds grapes from the hot house.

(opposite top) Amateur dramatics was a popular pastime for country house parties. In September 1904 'The Palace of Truth', by W.S.Gilbert was presented at Seend Manor. The event was organised by Mrs James MacKay to raise funds for the Church of the Holy Cross in the village.

(opposite bottom) There were not many occupations that men considered to be fit for Victorian ladies. Calling on friends and leaving cards occupied much time away from the running and ordering of the household while on Sunday, church services and visits to favoured tenants and parishioners filled the day. An acceptable outdoor game was croquet and it has clearly provided much amusement to these ladies pictured on their lawn near Trowbridge.

(left) A matronly lady is flanked by two splendid grandmothers in the village of Ham, c1905. The old ladies prefer the traditional sun bonnet (the country name for columbines is Granny's bonnets) while the younger wears a more modern hat. Despite a clothes line being in existence the washing is still spread over the bushes to dry.

(above) The country cottage of the Steven's family at Horton, c1905, was doubtless a homely and comfortable place to judge from the appearance of the ladies of the household. The cottage is timber framed with a good roof of thatch coming well down over the upper floor. The rent of such a home was about 5 shillings (25p) and a labourer's wage was about 15 shillings (75p) per week.

The nouveau riche of the towns tended to build and own large houses. The Croft, in Swindon, was the home of the Morse family who owned a big department store in the town. Between 1903 and 1910 the family held several conventions at their home and the sober and respectable citizens from one of these took a great deal of trouble to arrange themselves for the photographer.

Town Life

WILTSHIRE towns all have different characteristics and are most definitely distinct from one another. The only city is Salisbury, with its splendid cathedral and medieval street plan. Although a city it has all the characteristics of a good market town serving a large country area. Wilton is the ancient capital, a town which has given its name to the country and to the carpets manufactured there. Devizes is another true market town, serving a large area, and many of its industries are connected with agriculture.

Swindon was the railway town and is an excellent example of a place that grew large solely on one major industry. Wootton Bassett and Cricklade are ancient boroughs but were greatly overshadowed by the neighbouring, brash upstart called New Swindon. Another market town and old borough was Marlborough, but here a different aspect was the main London road from Bath and the west, the inns and hotels in the High Street testify to the number of travellers who stayed here overnight.

Malmesbury is a hilltop town, owing more to Gloucestershire and the Cotswolds than to Wiltshire, while Chippenham is a market and woollen town which developed an engineering industry. Corsham was supported by its stone quarries and the influence of Corsham Court while the ancient borough of Calne expanded with its bacon industry. Bradford on Avon, Melksham, Westbury, Warminster and Trowbridge were all market and woollen manufacturing towns which developed in different ways. Bradford, with its splendid hillside position, became a tourist attraction while Melksham supported the local rubber industry. Westbury became an important railway town while Warminster was home to the army. Trowbridge, largely by accident, became the administrative centre and also developed a food processing industry. It was also the final home of the Wiltshire woollen industry with the last mill, Samual Salter's, closing in 1982.

Despite the different purposes, these towns gave their inhabitants similar life patterns. It was a life of contrasts, where fine houses and gracious living rubbed shoulders with slum cottages and ragged children. Gradually public services were introduced, piped water, gas, sewerage systems, refuse disposal and electricity. The towns were lively, with people keenly interested in local affairs and the activities of their neighbours. Bustling and busy places, with their mills and markets, shops and inns, they were the metropolis of the country dweller.

The shop of John Alexander Brown in Bradford on Avon presented a splendid array of goods in 1893. There are many items to note in this view including the lawnmower, with grassbox, behind the cart, the very broad rakes and an interesting display of tin baths in the top floor window. The hip bath in the left hand window cost £1 while the bicycle below it was £10. Apart from the bearded gentleman, Mr Edmond Long a customer, all those pictured are members of staff; the shop owner stands behind the horse.

(above) A famous and familiar figure in Malmesbury was Harry Jones of The King's Arms. So well known was he that letters addressed merely with a drawing of his hat were correctly delivered to his hotel. Harry Jones was an exceptional landlord in being known throughout England, but mine host of the local inn was an important figure in the social life of any town.

(right) After the introduction of the penny post in 1840 many more families could afford to keep in touch with distant relatives than ever before. For those who could not write there was usually a neighbour who could take dictation and read aloud any incoming letters. By 1850, when this postman was photographed in Malmesbury he was a familiar and trusted figure in the streets. After making 2 deliveries each day this man spent his evenings as a bellringer at St Mary's Church.

(above left) The water supply of many households depended on the town pump. Most towns also had water carriers who hawked buckets of water to housewives who lived some distance from the pump. The Conigre Pump in Trowbridge was a well known landmark and was the object of attention for many American visitors, whose families had originated in the town. Some of them even wished to take it home as a souvenir. This posed picture is c1905 and is interesting for the washing, including the long combinations in the dormer window, hanging out to dry.

(below left) Floods were a common feature of life when rivers were less like drainage ditches and many towns possess metal plaques indicating record flood levels. This picture of Mill Street, Calne, shows the floods of April 9th 1920. The householders had to take to their upper floors and are seen anxiously regarding the swift flowing, wreckage strewn water.

(below) Declarations of election results were always well attended and excitement and conflict between rival interests was ever present, especially when the contest was expected to be so close that a recount would be demanded. Men wore their political colours (blue for a Conservative, red for a Liberal) proudly, and much earnest and sometimes outspoken debate took place. This declaration, at Swindon, for the Cricklade and North Wilts division was in June 1886. Mr N. Storey – Maskelyne, a Liberal Unionist, was returned despite the national landslide against the Liberals over the question of Irish Home Rule. The turnout here was 70%.

(above) Wiltshire towns were market towns and originally dpended to a great extent on the produce of the surrounding countryside. Markets were the main places for trading, meeting friends and hearing new ideas; often people travelled many miles to the chief ones. Their importance and number declined after both canals and railways made the movement of goods easy and cheap. Chippenham, pictured in the 1890s, was one of the survivors and held a cheese market once a month, a cattle market twice a month and a weekly corn market. There were also annual wool markets and cattle shows.

(right) A vital public service, not often photographed, was the dust cart which collected the increasingly large amounts of refuse produced by communities which were using greater quantities and more variety of goods than ever before. The Surveyor and Sanitary Inspector, Edwin Gunstone, was responsible for refuse collection in the Melksham Urban District Council area during the 1890s. This cart is pictured in Church Street, probably at the beginning of the day's round.

(left) The pedestrian filled thoroughfare is Regent Street, Swindon, at a time (1905) when there was little wheeled traffic other than the trams, which gave noisy warning of their approach. The Regent Arcade at this time contained small shops, in the 1920s it became the Arcadian Cinema. Many of the shops have their own large gas lamps while among the articles for sale are rubber garden hoses at the Swindon Rubber Depot.

(below) The shopfront of James Lott, 50 Regent Street, Swindon, contains a bewildering array of articles. Starting as an ironmonger, Mr Lott added many other lines including heating and electrical engineering. The firm also repaired scales in their Temple Street premises. Most items on display would find their counterparts in a modern ironmongers but the inclusion of candle and oil lamps with the gas mantles and electric light bulbs indicate the exciting, changing life of the early twentieth century. Shell Motor Spirit was also available at this well stocked emporium.

(right) The chemist's shop was a fascinating place, especially for children, with large glass jars full of strange liquids and powders. Many people, when ill, would visit the chemist rather than the doctor and the patient's waiting room in this shop was up the stairs on the right. Among the special offers at this chemists in Wood Street, Swindon, c1904, were packets of lemonade crystals, for 2½d (1p), which would make up to two gallons. Items such as throat pastilles were sold loose from the jars on the left.

(below) The staff at the Fleet Street premises of H. Freeth & Son, the Swindon grocers, c1903. The sides of Wiltshire bacon each weighed 60lbs and could be purchased 'mild cured' at 6d (2½p) a pound. The hygenic white coats of the assistants contrast strangely with the practice of hanging unwrapped food in the street.

(left) The well stocked interior of John Chapman's china shop in Fore Street, Trowbridge, c1906. The chamber pots are discreetly stacked under the counter while that most Victorian of objects, the jardinière, stands in the centre foreground. A 50 piece dinner service cost around £1 while a set of 3 jugs, hanging on the left, was 1/3d (6p).

(below) Marlborough High Street, in 1867, presents a very quiet scene with a cockerell strolling along the gutter. Number 125 High Street later became the Capital and Counties Bank with a new building in 1871. It is now Lloyd's Bank.

(right) The fire engine was a familiar part of town life. This engine, pictured at Chippenham by the railway arches in 1899, was a Merryweather Carriage Fire Engine purchased in 1849 for the sum of £96. Many of the fires dealt with involved hay ricks but the manual appliance was also used for several house fires.

(below) Milk deliveries by handcart or horsedrawn float were common in the early twentieth century; milk being sold direct from the churn. The Percy family of Salisbury contained 4 dairymen in 1907 and the carts shown here are at the Hamilton Road premises of William Percy. The small milk cans on the carts were for customers who had forgotten their own while a long handled ladle was used for transferring the milk from the churn. The Wyndham Dairy also produced their own butter and were proud to advertise it as being 'fresh daily'.

(above) Markets for Wiltshire cheese existed at both Chippenham and Salisbury. The latter market lapsed around 1900 but during the nineteenth century it was a regular event on the second Thursday in each month. In the 1850s and 1860s one cheese factor was Mr Arnold, in the white coat. To his right Mr Edward Simper, a cheese merchant, talks to Mr Rider, a lay reader at St Pauls. The picture is completed by a shepherd who is watching the weighing. The retail value of a pound of cheese was 10d (4p).

(below) The horsedrawn wagon of W.H.Milton, who provided fried fish and chip potatoes cooked over a charcoal brazier, was a familiar sight to Trowbridge people. Operating from 41 Shail's Lane, he provided a service of 'quality and cleanliness' in the streets and at local fairs, fetes and markets. This picture is c1907; in later years his daughter Mary, seen here leading the horse, became very well known when she carried on the family business.

(above) The grocer's shop was nearly always well stocked with attractive displays. Pickles, sauces, spices and salt are the main features of this Melksham window. The character standing by the Edwardian letter box, c1907, is Little John Chapman who used to accost passers by asking, 'How did I get like this?'. He became a local celebrity because of his size and lived to the age of 67, being looked after by his sister.

(right) One of the largest markets in the county was at Salisbury. In 1860 the market seems to be fairly chaotic with none of the livestock pens which were to appear later in the century. This view shows that the camera used did not provide great depth of field as the cattle and wagon in the foreground are sharp but the rest of the picture is out of focus. The long time required for the exposure of the photographic plate is also evident as there is a great deal of movement.

(below) The hub of town life was the market and while Swindon's development came too late for an interest in livestock, the general market was very popular. The buildings, containing 17 shops, were erected at the bottom of Commercial Road in 1892 at a cost of £4,500. The triangular piece of open ground was for the use of country dealers and sometimes contained 80 stalls. This picture is c1900, in 1903 the whole market was covered.

Craftsmen and Industry

THE traditional industry of Wiltshire, from medieval times, had been the weaving and finishing of woollens. By the beginning of the nineteenth century this had died out in all but the western parts of the county. Here steam power provided the basis for a transition from a cottage industry to a factory system between 1800 and 1850. Compared to its Yorkshire counterpart, however, the Wiltshire industry was slow to introduce new machinery and adapt to changing fashions and so suffered in the competition between the two areas.

The new technology of the mills created a need for mill engineers, and an early example was George Haden who installed steam engines in Trowbridge for Boulton & Watt, found the town to his liking, and settled there. The firm later became famous for its central heating systems and its installations provided the heating for such buildings as the British Museum and Westminster Abbey. Other engineering works included, Rowland Brotherhood (railway rolling stock) and various firms making railway signals at Chippenham, and Spencers at Melksham. Devizes became the centre for the manufacture of mobile steam engines while important agricultural machinery works were sited at Warminster, Bratton and Devizes.

Food processing, with bacon, milk and cheese predominating had made Wiltshire well known. Rubber manufacture began at Bradford on Avon in 1848 with Stephen Moulton but later moved to Melksham in 1889. Brewing was mainly undertaken by the landlords of the inns and in 1867 there were 95 brewers. The major breweries began to swallow the smaller and by 1903 there were only 65. During the nineteenth century tanning became a factory system with J. & T. Beaven at Holt, Ware Bros at Salisbury, and many others, while gloving firms included Boulton Bros. and A.L. & W.L. Jefferies, both of Westbury, and Chas. Ockwell of Cricklade.

Paper has been made, using the water from the clear streams, since the sixteenth century while one of the earliest snuff factories in the country was E. & W. Anstie Ltd. of Devizes. The firm later also produced shag tobacco and cigarettes. Snuff was also ground in Bradford on Avon, giving that town the nickname of 'Snuffy'.

Wiltshire was an important area for the production of Bath stone. Quarries at Box, Corsham and Bradford on Avon have been responsible for the stone used in many important buildings. Other rocks have provided, Portland stone, flint for building, chalk for lime and quick lime, clay for bricks and sand. There are also iron ore deposits at Seend and Westbury. The former were worked between 1856 and 1889 while the latter operted from 1857 to 1925.

Although there was a large variety of industries it is important to remember that most people's livelihood was still connected with the land. It should also be realized that there were large numbers of craftsmen – carpenters, wheelwrights, thatchers, ropemakers, cobblers, clock makers, blacksmiths, and many more who worked throughout the county.

(above left) The First World War brought prosperity to many businesses and towns. At Chippenham, Saxby & Farmers (later to become Westinghouse) were producing munitions. It is interesting to note that of the 20 workers in the milling section there are only 3 men, the rest were in the armed forces and their places had been taken by women, many of them employed for the first time.

(above right) Workers pictured at the Waterford Cloth Mills, of Rawlings & Pocock at Chippenham, hold shuttles from their power looms, c1912. By this time English wool was no longer used, supplies being imported from Australia, and although the West of England cloth trade was in decline it still excelled in the finishing processes and produced the finest raised cloths in the country.

(middle right) The Melksham firm of C. W. Maggs & Co. was founded in 1803 and manufactured mats, rope, and twine. The ropes were originally used in the Somerset coalfields while the coir matting, being made on this loom, was a later development. The 3 matmakers, Charles Park, Alfred Redman and Sam Gulley, totalled 168 years of service to the company between them. The business had its factory and rope works by the canal bridge in Spa Road.

(bottom right) Two cutting machines in the cloth mills of Palmer & MacKays at Trowbridge, c1900. These were used for trimming the cloth, after the nap had been raised, a job which had been previously done by hand using a large (between 5 and 6 feet long) pair of shears. It was from the early cutting machines that the lawnmower was developed.

Women wind bobbins at Palmer & MacKay's woollen mill in Trowbridge at the turn of the century. Overhead is a complicated system of belting which transmitted power throughout the factory. It was this form of power transmission that created many problems at this period.

The West Wiltshire woollen industry became increasingly mechanized as the nineteenth century progressed. Weaving had always been carried on in the home of the weaver using a narrow handloom as shown. Weaver's houses are identifiable by the large north facing windows on the top floor and whole streets of them were built in towns between 1790 and 1830. By the 1840s power looms were in use and handloom weaving died out by the 1870s. This loom was photographed at Palmer & MacKay's factory at Trowbridge in 1903 and it was probably only used for training and displays.

(right) As the nineteenth century moved on towards its close fewer public houses brewed their own beer and many became tied houses of local breweries. These breweries were subject to mergers and take overs and by 1900 there was only one in most Wiltshire towns. The dominant names were Wadworths of Devizes, Ushers of Trowbridge, Arkells of Swindon and Gibbs Mew of Salisbury. At Bradford on Avon Wilkins Bros. were not only brewers and maltsters but also manufactured mineral waters and retailed wines and spirits.

(below) Two photographs of the works of John Hall & Co. of Warminster have been joined with reasonable accuracy to produce a panoramic view. Many of the staff are pictured, including some who had been with the company for 50 years. The firm began manufacturing paints at the end of the 1860s.

(above) Apart from Scout Motors at Salisbury, the motor car was not manufactured in Wiltshire. However many firms opened garages for the sale and repair of the new vehicles; Barnes Bros. already ran a steam roller works at Southwick when they opened this garage in Trowbridge. The car, AM 1119 on the left, was a Darracq registered by Sarah Barnes of Southwick in December 1907, while the vehicle on the right, AM 2041, was an Arral – Johnston Torpedo registered by Barnes Bros.

(right) Mill fires were common because the minute woollen fibres which escaped into the atmosphere were very inflammable. Most mills caught fire at one time or another, Waterford Mill at Chippenham, which was built in 1811, survived until 1915 when a disasterous fire on May 22nd destroyed much of the factory. The firemen who fought the blaze are pictured among the debris.

(left) The north west of Wiltshire is good limestone country and several quarries have been worked over the centuries. At Corsham much of the stone was quarried underground, preferably in the winter, and kept underground until the weather became milder. It was then 'seasoned' on the surface during the summer. This helped prevent decay but towards the end of the nineteenth century stone was in such demand that it was used without being sufficiently weathered; the results can be seen by looking at stone houses built at this time. The stone in the Worked Stone Yard, in 1890, is probably being cut soon after quarrying.

Many small towns and villages supported several industries. The business of R. & J. Reeves, agricultural implement manufacturers of Bratton, was well known while at Pewsey the local agricultural engineers and iron founders were Whatley & Co. of the High Street. This picture of the interior of their premises, c 1900, shows sand being cleared away after the casting of an iron wheel.

As the woollen industry declined new uses were found for the empty mills. At Staverton the National Anglo-Swiss Milk Co. (now Nestlés) took over the splendid 1825 stone factory for use as a milk condensery. This 1905 picture, with the company's work girls, shows the mill with the full glory of its 6 storeys; during the 1930s it was unfortunately reduced to two.

The flint knapper had been a fairly common feature of the chalklands, producing small pieces of flint for flintlock guns or shaping stone for building. Edward Simpson, alias Flint Jack, brought a new dimension to this craft. He had been a servant in Whitby, Yorkshire, to both an historian and a geologist, and had developed a great interest in, and understanding of, fossils and flint implements. He had a genuine craftsman's appreciation of stone implements and became one of the few men of the nineteenth century to understand and work flint in the same way as prehistoric man. Unfortunately the scientific implications of his knowledge were not understood and the Victorian love of collecting objects, rather than studying them, proved to be his undoing.

For some years he made a reasonable living fabricating fossils and flints and when photographed in 1863 had been making a series of flints to order for Edward Stevens, Honourary Curator of the Blackmore Museum in Salisbury. Although he never tried to pass off his flints as genuine to any serious historian, the collectors he had duped became outraged by what they saw as an attack on their pride and knowledge. Flint Jack's downfall came swiftly, aided by drink and burglary. It is sad to think that a century later he would have been regarded as an experimental archaeologist and would not have needed to sell his fake flints and fossils in order to eat.

Travel – by Road, Water and Air

IN 1840 the two basic ways of travelling were by road and water; in Wiltshire water meant the canals as the rivers were not navigable. For much of our period road travel was by horse drawn vehicles, or for most people on their own two feet. Despite improvements made by the turnpike trusts many country roads were in a poor state of repair and some became impassable at times during the winter. It is reputed that MacAdam himself was employed to resurface roads at Devizes, Warminster and Salisbury, but many roads remained as chalk and gravel tracks. In lowland north and west Wiltshire the roads over the clay were especially bad.

A wide range of horsedrawn vehicles used these routes from the stage coach to the donkey and cart. Local carriers and wagoners were among the most frequent users. When steam and motor traffic appeared in the late nineteenth and early twentieth centuries the main roads were resurfaced and often completely reconstructed.

The two main canals of Wiltshire, the Kennet and Avon and the Wilts and Berks, brought coal and building materials to many, once remote, parts of the county. From 1841 they were faced by competition from the railways and gradually faded as commercial, goods-carrying enterprises.

Air transport had little effect on Wiltshire, apart from creating a sense of wonderment at these flimsy, heavier-than-air machines that could actually carry men aloft. When one chanced to land in a field it was immediately surrounded by an admiring, fascinated crowd. The First World War made aeroplanes familiar to many more people and they became a common sight in Wiltshire. Balloon ascents also attracted much attention and admiration for the intrepid balloonists who were taken wherever the wind blew.

The spread of railways meant the death of canals although some, such as the Kennet and Avon, were well used for pleasure boating. The Wilts and Berks canal, seen here in Swindon from the Fleet Street bridge, is very weed choked in 1900 and has clearly not seen the passage of a boat for some time. The towpath is well used by pedestrians as is evidenced by the fact that it was considered worthwhile to place advertising hoardings on the canalside.

(above) In 1890 the Kennet and Avon canal, near Bradford on Avon, was still fairly clear and some commercial traffic, such as this horse drawn barge, was using the waterway. This canal also became well used for pleasure trips in the 1890s and early twentieth century.

(left) From the 1870s and the popularisation of the penny farthing, cycling became a widely enjoyed pastime. In the 1880s the safety bicycle, costing £7.10.0d (£7.50), appeared and cycling became much easier. When this picture of the Chippenham Wheelers was taken in the early twentieth century new bicycles cost £12 but had been produced in such numbers that many were available secondhand.

(above) The first motorised delivery vehicle of J. E. Evans & Sons, the Trowbridge Grocers. The vehicle, a 20 h.p. Ford 7 cwt van, was registered in December 1915. Its predecessor was a covered delivery wagon drawn by two horses.

(above right) Summer outings into the country were very popular with many families and before the coming of the motorised charabanc, a four-in-hand was the only way of transporting a large number of people. The Boulton and Routledge families, from Highworth, are seen at the outset of their trip on a slightly overloaded coach, c1904.

(middle right) A horse drawn van of the West Wilts Laundry, of Holt, c1910. The laundry covered a big area of Wiltshire and the surrounding counties with large houses and institutions being the chief customers. One Holt resident remembers that homing pigeons were also carried and released at the farthest point from the village, as a free service to pigeon fanciers on the part of the sympathetic proprietor.

(bottom right) A novel form of transport for a young lady could be seen in The Close at Salisbury in the early twentieth century. Mr W. Sewill, a local pawnbroker, fitted a small wheeled basket chair to the rear of his Minerva Motorcycle in order to take his daughter around the city.

During the 25 years of operation for Swindon's tramways only one serious accident occurred. In 1906, for the first time, the Bath and West and Southern Counties Show was held in the town and the car which left Wood Street, just before 7.00 p.m. on Friday 1st June, was crowded. At Wood Street it appeared that the driver was having some difficulty with the controls and on the steep gradient of Victoria Hill the tram quickly gathered speed. At the foot of the hill the tram hit the points and crashed onto its side striking a horsedrawn cab. Five people died and 30 were injured. The Corporation accepted full liability and eventually £24,404 was paid out to the bereaved and injured.

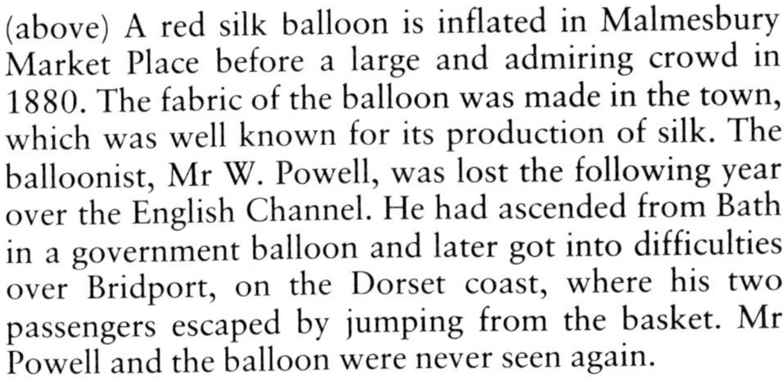

(above) A red silk balloon is inflated in Malmesbury Market Place before a large and admiring crowd in 1880. The fabric of the balloon was made in the town, which was well known for its production of silk. The balloonist, Mr W. Powell, was lost the following year over the English Channel. He had ascended from Bath in a government balloon and later got into difficulties over Bridport, on the Dorset coast, where his two passengers escaped by jumping from the basket. Mr Powell and the balloon were never seen again.

(above right) Repairs of roads and bridges within a parish were normally a local responsibility. At Castle Eaton, in the north of the county, men are at work in 1890 repairing an unstable looking bridge on the River Thames. The gentleman on the right is seemingly the surveyor or architect responsible.

(middle right) Two of the carriages belonging to Clark Bros., who were agents and carriers for the Great Western Railway at Cricklade. They also ran a passenger service between Purton and Cricklade until just after the First World War. Both vehicles are equipped with carriage lamps.

(bottom right) An early foot propelled invalid carriage, known as a dandy horse, was owned by this Melksham man in 1906. The picture was taken in the Market Place with the town pump, Town Hall and police station in the background.

In Swindon the Wilts and Berks canal lies neglected and rubbish – strewn, in the town which waxed fat on its successor the Great Western Railway. Another new form of transport, the tram, crosses the Fleet Street bridge. Swindon tramways had been opened in 1904 with a total length of 3 miles, 5 furlongs of track and 9 trams operating on an overhead trolley system. Among the advertisements on the tram is one for the newly opened (1910) cinema, the Electra Palace.

(above) By 1760 a dense network of turnpike roads had been built up in Wiltshire; the last road to be turnpiked in the county was in 1840. The improved roads led to more frequent and faster coach travel. The roads were maintained out of the tolls collected from the users at gates and houses such as these at Highworth. The uniformed toll gate keeper is on the right in this 1860 scene. Before the coming of the railways, a coach left the King and Queen Inn at 7.00 a.m. on Thursday and arrived in London at 4.00 a.m. on Saturday.

(right) Eight years after the first successful flight of the Wright brothers, and only two years after Bleriot had flown the English Channel, this machine landed in a field near Dauntsey in 1911. With most of the people only accustomed to agricultural machinery, the railways, and early motor cars, great interest was shown in this weird, fragile contraption.

(above) After the invention of the internal combustion engine many churches and clubs organised outings by charabanc. The charabanc, often with solid wheels, would carry passengers who were enjoying one of their few opportunities to take a holiday. This outing of 1912 was for the Highworth branch of the Royal Antediluvian Order of Buffaloes.

(left) One of the great innovations for the working man was the safety bicycle. If he could save the money for the initial purchase he was able to have his own transport which did not need expensive hay or petrol. The Pewsey cycle shop of G.E. Goddard is pictured c1920; in the window is an advertisement for Wiltshire made Avon tyres. Mr Goddard had formed the Pewsey Cycling Club at the turn of the century and was one of the instigators of the well known Pewsey Carnival. The carnival float entered by Goddards included many spectacularly decorated bicycles.

The Railways

Two railway companies built their lines in Wiltshire, The Great Western Railway and the London & Southampton Railway. The former used Brunel's broad gauge of 7 ft. ¼in. As far as the railway was concerned the county was merely an intermediate area between its termini and it was not until 1844, with the proposals of the Wiltshire, Somerset & Weymouth Railway, that there was any interest in serving local needs. Although all the major lines had been constructed by the 1860s the building of branch lines continued into the twentieth century..

One of the major engineering works was Box Tunnel, which at nearly two miles in length, is the longest in Britain. At the peak time of its construction 4,000 men and 300 horses were employed and on completion in 1841 it had cost £13 million. The broad gauge was found to be impractical where it met the standard gauge of other companies and sadly it was gradually phased out. The final changeover came at the end of May, 1892, when 3,400 men converted the remaining 171 miles of track in a single weekend.

The siting of the G.W.R. works at Swindon provided the main interest although several firms at Chippenham were also making railway equipment, especially signals. All Wiltshire towns and many villages were served and the opportunities for increased mobility were taken up by many people.

The social effects of the railway system were to be far reaching. In urban areas railway development was accompanied by the rise of a business and industrial middle class who were to take political power away from the landowners. In rural areas the social structure, with the squire at the top, remained. Even here though anyone disatisfied with his position in life was in easy reach of the large cities for the first time in English history. With sufficient motivation and energy anyone could get to a city and attempt to better themselves. Many countrymen did and the railway lines carried badly needed fresh blood into the industrial cities of the 19th century. Of course the railways not only provided transport for workers seeking fresh jobs but also gave people the opportunity to visit far flung relatives and take short holidays. The railways benefitted city and town dwellers in particular through the improvements to their diet as a result of the train's ability to transport perishable goods such as fresh milk and vegetables.

(opposite top) Nearly all G.W.R. traffic was controlled from their divisional office at Bristol, although between 1906 and 1910 an assistant superintendant worked at Westbury to maintain closer liason with Wiltshire. During the First World War Westbury was the natural centre for military movements in the Salisbury Plain area. To supervise this a fully equipped control office was built in 1916 and Westbury became an important railway town. All the main lines are shown in this picture, c1920.

(opposite bottom) One of the best known of all broad gauge engines built at Swindon was 'Lord of the Isles', a Great Western Railway Courier class. The engine had completed 780,000 miles with the same boiler on its withdrawal from service in 1884. The church of St Mark, in the background, was the parish church of New Swindon and also the railway church. It had been erected by the Great Western Railway between 1843 and 1845 at a cost of £5,500.

(top right) In the mid nineteenth century 4 attempts were made to bring a railway line to the town of Malmesbury. Success was achieved in 1877 when the line was finally opened. This picture, of 1876, shows work in progress with a coffee pot engine being used to carry hard core and rubble while the line is being laid.

(middle right) Brunel's broad gauge became difficult to operate and between June and August 1874 a third line was laid between Thingley Junction and Salisbury so that mixed traffic could use the line. In practice few broad gauge engines were used, the majority of the traffic being the standard gauge of 4 feet 8½ inches. This scene at Melksham Station is probably from June 1874.

An interior view of the Great Western Railway works at Swindon. Power is transmitted horizontally along the top of the workshops and transferred to machines and lathes by a system of belts.

Everyone travelled by train, including royalty. The mayor of Salisbury greets Edward VII on Brunel's all – over roofed station, where the flags, red carpet and potted plants divert the eye from the metal columns and girders. On the right is W. H. Smith's station bookstall where, apart from books and magazines, travellers could purchase postcards of Stonehenge and the Cathedral and travelling rugs and caps.

(right) One of the most serious accidents in Wiltshire was at Salisbury Station on Sunday 1st July 1906. The Plymouth to London boat train, which was said to travel through the city at 60 m.p.h., was derailed with the loss of 27 lives. Many of those killed were Americans, and most were in the dining car. This picture shows the work undertaken to clear the wreckage from the lines.

(below) Railway stations employed large numbers of staff. At Devizes in 1891 there were booking clerks and many porters under the stationmaster. There would also have been platelayers and gangers, the former laying and repairing the road, the latter walking their length daily looking for signs of wear, soil erosion and subsidence.

(above) The railway not only killed trade on canals and roads but threw its bridges and viaducts across these earlier ways of travelling. In 1906, at Cricklade, this cast iron bridge was erected to carry a branch line. With the girls in the foreground is a splendidly decorated pram.

(left) Swindon rapidly became the largest town in Wiltshire after it was selected as the site of the Great Western Railway works. By the early twentieth century more than 14,000 people were employed and it was regarded as one of the largest undertakings in British industry. This view of the Paint Shop is from 1885 and shows engines in various stages of completion.

Leisure Pursuits

THE concept of leisure was to most people a new and revolutionary one, and the activities you could engage in, varied greatly depending on your station in life. The majority of people had little free time and needed to spend it in rest, sleep or producing food, rather than expending energy in, what were to them, useless pursuits. There were however many countrymen who poached and fished not only for the pot, but because they enjoyed the sport.

For those people who had a reasonable amount of spare time, the nineteenth century provided more activities to fill them than had ever been available before. Sports included football, cricket, tennis and croquet, as well as the more purposeful hunting, shooting and fishing. With the invention of the bicycle cycling became a popular pastime, and at this time many sports were organized with their own regional and national associations.

Collecting was a Victorian passion and few subjects escaped their eager aquisitiveness. The introduction of self adhesive postage stamps in 1840, opened up the wide and varied field of philately while those with more expensive tastes indulged themselves in paintings, sculptures, first editions of books and antiquities. Many ephemeral items were collected; heraldic letter headings and later picture postcards were both very popular. Natural history provided many topics with pressed flowers, ferns, butterflies, birds eggs, and even stuffed birds and animals.

Many gentlemen occupied themselves with an early form of archaeology, but much of this had consisted only of opening up barrows of an afternoon and seeing what treasures lay buried within. Serious archaeology developed with the century and for its followers became a life work rather than a leisure pursuit. Wiltshire is rich in prehistoric remains and has produced many good archaeologists, including B.H. and Maud Cunnington who discovered and excavated many sites, including All Cannings Cross, for the Wiltshire Archaeological and Natural History Society. This society was formed in 1853 and, based at its museum in Devizes, has always been very active in promoting archaeology in the county.

Indoor amusements were seldom photographed but they occupied many family evenings. The evenings of music, song and recitation are well known but charades, amateur dramatics, cards and board games were also very popular. The activities of the many societies and organizations that were formed could also come under the heading of indoor leisure, although those that were interested in studying such subjects as geology, flora or architecture made many field trips into the countryside.

For those who had the time to spare there were plenty of activities to fill it. Many pursuits combined both a hobby or interest with a useful end product. All forms of needlework are a good example of this, and the cottager who was interested in producing his own vegetables had not only food but also home made wine.

Holidays as such were not often available to most Wiltshire people although the railways and charabancs enabled many to enjoy a day at Weston Super Mare or Weymouth. Later the factories began to close down for a week which enabled some families to take a week's holiday. The best known was Swindon's Trip Week when the whole G.W.R. works closed down.

The protection and restoration of old buildings had become a popular leisure pursuit for the middle classes after William Morris had founded The Society for the Protection of Ancient Buildings. This picture shows the start of the restoration of Malmesbury Abbey, undertaken by Harold Brakspear in 1899. It was completed in 1912 and transformed part of the Abbey into Malmesbury's parish church.

Electioneering provided a means of occupying leisure time for some people. One of the issues which brought about a Liberal landslide in the 1906 Elections was the question of Chinese Labour on the Rand gold reefs of the South African Transvaal. Balfour's administration had allowed the importation of 100,000 Chinese into South Africa and a mixture of fear of the Yellow Peril and sympathy for the victims of capitalism swept the country. In Melksham the issue provoked this procession of workmen from Maggs' factory in support of Fuller, the Liberal candidate. Unfortunately after the new government had been elected to office no action was taken on the matter for some years.

(right) The spread of golf was fairly rapid but it was not until April 11th 1907 that the West Wilts Club was opened at Warminster. The ceremony was performed by Mr A. J. Balfour, at that time leading the Conservative Opposition in the Commons, who is seen driving off from the first tee.

The Bear Field, at Melksham, was the scene of many sporting and social events. On this occasion, in the 1890s, it was the venue for a penny farthing race which ended with a very close finish. Racing on these machines, and on a grass track, must have been very uncomfortable.

(left) Leisure pursuits connected with the church were some of the few free activities available to the townsman, and his children were catered for by the Sunday School. The picture shows a Congregational Church Sunday School Rally in Melksham Market Place in 1886.

(right) Football was first recorded in Wiltshire in the early seventeenth century and the oldest recognised club in the county was Holt who were formed in 1864. This team from nearby Melksham were playing in 1890, sporting a wide variety of jerseys and an apparent lack of shin pads.

(below) Betting took place surreptitiously and bookmakers often operated from pubs and barbers where they were hidden from the law. Runners were also employed to collect betting slips during the day. Pay outs to the lucky winners were often made on a round of the pubs in the evening. The power of the law retaliated at Sherston in 1912 when bookmakers were raided and their equipment confiscated at a race meeting.

Bands were very popular and many towns and villages had their brass or silver band. The Malmesbury Town Band, resplendent in their uniforms were photographed in 1880.

(above) The Bible Class and Reading Party were typical products of the Victorian and Edwardian church. These usually consisted of young men such as these in Mr Humphries' Bible Class at Wootton Bassett.

(right) Archaeology was a popular pastime at all levels. In Salisbury a gravel pit on the edge of Milford Hill cricket ground provided the site where, in 1864, a 'good flint implement' was found. The exact location is being shown to the lady by the local archaeologist while the workman takes a well earned rest from the digging.

(above) Many landowners and professional men had undertaken archaeological excavations and it was a Wiltshire landowner, General Pitt Rivers, who laid the foundations and principles of modern archaeology. The excavations at Stonehenge in 1901 were directed by Professor William Gowland, seen examining a possible find in one of the sieves. A series of these sieves with meshes of 1 inch, 1/2 inch, 1/4 inch and 1/8 inch were used so that no object, however small, would be lost.

(right) Village rivalries often came out in football matches at the time of public holidays, these occasions having originated in the massed and bloody events where whole villages turned out and played with their village centres as the goals. Although this had died out, a residue remained in the form of properly organised matches at Christmas and Easter. At the latter festival the married men of North Bradley played the single men for a barrel of beer provided by the landlord of the Rising Sun. Pictured are some of the players, c1908.

High Days and Holidays

OCCURRENCES of local and national festivity provided high spots in an existence that was otherwise fairly routine and monotonous. The most obvious and well photographed examples are Queen Victoria's Jubilees and the Coronations of Edward VII and George V. Many towns put on elaborate dinners and processions and most communities enjoyed an ox roast or jollification of some description. The Victorians delighted in extensive menus and many provincial newspapers contain long accounts of dinners and the amounts of food and drink consumed.

At other times some royal or noble personage would visit a town and decorations and flags would lend an air of gaiety to the otherwise familiar scene. Some villages had their own customs and festivals, Oak Apple Day at Great Wishford, the Duck Feast (to commemorate poet Stephen Duck) at Charlton, and the Aldbourne Feast among many others. These were eagerly anticipated for weeks beforehand.

Victory in wars, such as the Crimean or South African, were a cause of local rejoicing, especially the latter as the Wiltshire Regiment were involved. Another national event which provoked much local involvement was Parliamentary elections. Political feelings ran high and electioneering, particularly if there was any profit in it by way of free drinks and dinners, was a welcome activity.

Local events also gave opportunities for celebration. Flower Shows, the birth of a son and heir to the lord of the manor, and the annual dinners of organizations all provided something to look forward to, and a topic of conversation for weeks after the event. The coming of the railway, piped water, gas or electricity were all marked by ceremonies and dinners, in fact public dinners were used for recording every possible event!

The Diamond Jubilee of Queen Victoria, in 1897, was celebrated by roasting oxen in many towns and villages. The Wesley Road Liberal Club in Trowbridge, a town with a tradition of pork butchers, differed and held a pig roast at the rear of their premises.

The longevity of the Queen and the certainty of an Empire on which the sun never set were excellent reasons for public celebration. In Wiltshire this was recorded by dinners, processions and the erection of enormous floral arches. The Cross Hayes in Malmesbury was used for a dinner to mark the Golden Jubilee in 1887. In this picture the feast is coming to an end and some of the tables have been cleared. The month is June and the umbrellas have not been opened for protection against the rain, but against the sun, for this was a very hot day and it was not fashionable for Victorian ladies to have sunburned faces.

(above) The festivities for Queen Victoria's Diamond Jubilee included a show of music and military might in Marlborough. A guard of honour fronts the Town Hall while a regimental band provides entertainment for the flag carrying townspeople.

(right) The traditional way of celebrating an important event, whether it was the birth of a son to a local landowner or a royal jubilee, was by means of an ox roast. At Melksham the 1897 Diamond Jubilee was celebrated thus with local butchers officiating.

(this page and opposite page) The Coronation of King Edward VII provided the opportunity to hold many civic celebrations. In Salisbury these included carnival processions through the streets with floats from organisations and areas of the city. In the Market Place a public dinner was held for 4,000 men. The whole event was organized by a group of committees supervised by Mr Salter – the Beverage Committee, photographed in front of the Council House, were responsible for the 800 gallons of beer drunk. Apart from bottled beer there were barrels set up all around the Market Place, those on the right of the picture of the dinner are painted white, probably in an attempt to keep the beer cool by reflecting the sun's rays. This was a much photographed event and an unattended plate camera can be seen in the foreground. The ladies were catered for separately at an afternoon tea in Victoria Park where a ton of cake and 50lbs of tea were consumed. The love of public feasting, inherited from the nineteenth century, was dying however and only one more was held in Salisbury, the Coronation feast for George V in 1911.

(left) The ancient town of Malmesbury decorated its fine octagonal market cross for the Coronation of Edward VII. Hanging all over the structure are small coloured glass jars, containing candles which were lighted on the evening of Coronation Day. The jars in the centre form the letters 'E R' either side of a crown.

(below) The entire village of Imber, on Salisbury Plain, is gathered together to celebrate the Coronation of King George V in 1911. The village was able to enjoy one more coronation before all 47 families were evacuated in 1943 when the War Office took over their village for use as a training ground.

(above) Souvenir mugs are commonplace now but in 1911 they were a great curiosity to these children of Calne. The occasion was the Coronation of King George V, which Calne celebrated with many events including a horse parade. The tin baths behind the dais are still full of mugs, a fact which indicates that the proceedings have just begun with the youngest children.

(right) A high spot of the year was the Christmas live meat display. In Trowbridge, Garlicks' show for the year 1900 featured 18 beasts including the Hereford steer in the foreground. This animal came from Queen Victoria's herd and had been purchased at Smithfield Market. These shows are such an important part of the Christmas celebrations that few people minded the main street being blocked for some hours.

(above) In July 1907 King Edward VII and Queen Alexandra visited Bowood as guests of the Marquis of Lansdowne. Before leaving from Calne railway station the royal couple were presented with an Address from the Borough of Calne at the Town Hall. Everyone was in their best clothes and the festivities were to be completed by sports and other events but unfortunately rain storms caused these to be postponed.

(left) Election time provided an opportunity for high jinks and mischief, politics were most vigorously debated and practical jokes played on one another by the rival parties. In Wootton Bassett Mr Ernest Camden, a general dealer, is electioneering with his donkey and cart. The pig under the netting is painted blue. The result of the 1910 election for this North Wilts division was a victory for Col. Calley, the Unionist candidate, by a majority of 635.

The Armed Forces

THE main impact of the army was in the military occupation of Salisbury Plain. Starting with the purchase of the 364 acres of Grove Farm in 1897 the War Department, by 1902, owned 43,500 acres. The effects were immense. Many areas became prohibited and some villages, such as Tidworth, were transformed into small garrison towns. Other villages affected were Bulford, Larkhill and Durrington.

During the First World War the Plain was visited by most British regiments and many from the Dominions. Many are commemorated by their badges, cut into the white chalk as were the famous white horses a century earlier. After the war regular training was resumed and some of the land on the fringes of the army area was leased out to farmers.

The Wiltshire Regiment, as such, was formed in 1881 by the amalgamation of the 62nd (Wiltshire) Regiment and the 99th (The Duke of Edinburgh's) Regiment. A regimental depot had been established at Le Marchant Barracks, Devizes, in 1878 and the Wiltshires were based there. They had already seen service in the Crimea and India and now fought in South Africa during the Boer War from 1899 to 1902.

In the First World War battalions of the Regiment saw action at Mons, Neuve Chapelle and Ypres before the onset of trench warfare. Other battalions were involved at Gallipoli and Salonika. Three battalions were in the battle of the Somme while other Wiltshiremen saw service in Egypt, Turkey and Mesopotamia.

As well as the Wiltshire Regiment the Volunteers and Militia provided opportunities for military service and militiamen were welcome recruits to the Regiment for they were well known for their soundness as soldiers. Many a country lad must have found the King's shilling preferable to his staid life although many probably regretted their choice later.

Officers of the Wiltshire Militia pictured at Warminster in 1867. The Militia was under the command of Col., The Marquis of Ailesbury while among the captains were the Earl of Suffolk and Lord H. Thynne.

(opposite top) The marching song of the Wiltshire Regiment was 'The Vly (be on the turnip)', a tune much played by the Regimental Band pictured here at Devizes.

(opposite bottom) The 2nd Battalion of the Wiltshire Regiment did not return to this country after the Boer War until 1903. In this picture men of the Cyclist Section take a break during manoeuvres. The 2nd Battalion went on to serve at Pembroke Dock and in Ireland until the outbreak of the First World War.

With a large military presence on Salisbury Plain, many villages were surrounded by army ranges and training grounds. One such was Imber, an isolated village put into verse thus, 'Imber on the down, four miles from any town'. The 4 miles is a modest estimate and the community was frequently cut off in winter. In later times the village was prosperous with well tended gardens and tidy cottages, as can be seen from this 1910 photograph. Unfortunately the village was to suffer for its surrounding ranges, in 1943 the whole settlement was evacuated and the area used for D Day training. Despite a promise made to the villagers they were never allowed to come back to resume the life they knew. Today the village is dead, only the church and churchyard have survived more or less intact.

(above) Although Salisbury Plain had been taken over by the army, Wiltshire was to become home for bases of the Royal Flying Corps. Here cavalry officers obey the notice to keep back while an early machine of the R.F.C. is put through its paces.

(left) Social life for the military community was important. In 1896 this fancy dress donkey derby took place at Devizes. The costumes seem to owe their origins both to service in India and to Wiltshire rural life!

(above) Encouraging the morale of troops during the First World War was very important and one of the chief exponents was the indefatigable Queen Mary. This inspection is taking place at Palmer & MacKay's woollen mills in Trowbridge.

(right) The end of an era was marked in Trowbridge with the sight of these men training in the Park before joining up to fight in the First World War. The War Memorial, which now stands at the right hand end of this line of men, reminds us of the 300 who did not return to their native town.

(above) Trowbridge had been originally garrisoned to help quell local riots. A cavalry barracks was built in 1794 while further extensions were made during the Victorian period. Dominion troops were in the town during the First World War; this picture shows Australian troops marching from the Barracks along Newtown in 1918.

(opposite top) During the First World War many large houses were loaned or requisitioned for use as convalescent homes for wounded soldiers. Travancore House, at Pewsey, had been loaned to the Red Cross by the Hayward family and was staffed by volunteers from the Pewsey area. This picture, from Christmas 1914, shows members of the Voluntary Aid Detachment of the 14th Wiltshire Red Cross with some of their military patients.

(opposite bottom) The end of the First World War was an occasion of relief, as well as one of celebration, for most towns and villages had sent all their available manpower to the front. Those servicemen who returned from the war expected to find their efforts rewarded by a better standard of living for all. Many were disappointed, but at least they were remembered by local rolls of honour and by dinners, such as this one at Chippenham held on Peace Day, 1919, for men who had served in the armed forces.

Index of Places
by page number